E $8.69
Re   Reimold, Mary
             My mom is a runner

DATE DUE

AG 16 '91	AUG 09	JY 0 8 '19	
AP 23 '92	JUN 16		
MY 28 '92	JY 24 '00	AUG 09	
OC 14 '92			
JY 1 '96	AG 04 00		
	JE 26 01		
AUG 04	JE 28 02		
AUG 23 '98	JY 22 '02		
OCT 24 '98	JY 16 '07		
NOV 05	OC 1 0		
JUN 05			
AUG 09	2 3 '18		

DEMCO

My
Mom
Is a
RUNNER

To my husband
and sons, John and Nolan

My Mom Is a RUNNER

Mary Gallagher Reimold

Sid Dorris
photographer

Abingdon Press
Nashville

My Mom Is a Runner

Copyright © 1987 by Abingdon Press

Photography by Sid Dorris

book design and production by J S Laughbaum

Library of Congress Cataloging in Publication Data

Reimold, Mary Gallagher, 1953-
  My mom is a runner.

  Summary: A child is proud of his mother who runs.
  [1. Mothers—Fiction. 2. Running—Fiction] I. Dorris, Sid, ill. II. Title.
PZ7.R27467My 1987   [E]   97-1312

ISBN 0-687-27545-8 (alk. paper)

Printed in Hong Kong

My name is John and my mom is a runner.

Every morning after dressing me and my little
brother, Nolan, Mom fixes us breakfast.

Then she gets ready to run.

First she puts on her running clothes and does her stretching exercises.

When she puts on her sneakers, I know it is time for her to run.

After our babysitter, Juanita, arrives, Mom dashes out the door, but first she gives us both a kiss good-bye.

When my mom first started running, I didn't like
it. Just as she was leaving I would scream, "Don't
run, Mom!" But it didn't stop her. She would just
say, "I'll be back soon," and off she ran.

Mom says running is fun.

She runs in the rain,

in the snow,

in the wind,

up hills and down hills.

And she always runs back to us.

Sometimes my mom lets us run with her. She takes us to the track where we run around and around and around until we get tired.

While she continues to run, we rest in the
middle of the track field.

I'm glad my mom runs now and so is Nolan. I tell my friends how strong and fast she is. Not many kids have a mom who runs.

Sometimes Mom enters a race, and Dad takes us to watch her run.

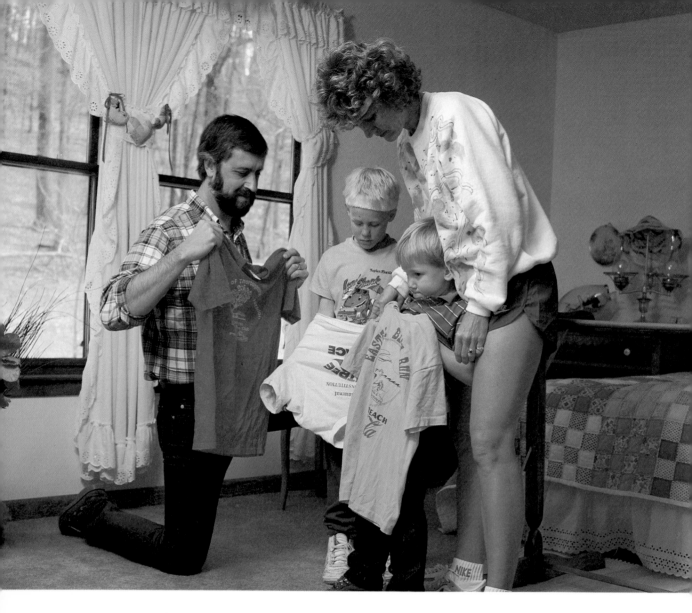

If she wins a trophy or gets a T-shirt, she lets us have it. She gives my dad shirts, too.

After each race we all go out for ice cream. I like that part of the race best!

Once my mom ran a marathon. Dad and Nolan
and I waited at the finish line for a really long time.

I started to worry so I asked my dad, "Where is Mom? Why isn't she here yet?"

He said marathons are twenty-six miles long and it takes a long time to finish.

When she finally arrived, we started to cheer and clap. I yelled, "Run, Mommy!"

She didn't win that race, but Dad gave her a gold medal anyway. He said anyone who finishes a marathon should get a gold medal.

One night after tucking me into bed, she said, "When you grow up and if you run a marathon, I'll give you this gold medal."

I hope one day I can run like my mom.